C
To The
Rescue

Written & Illustrated By
Steve Daniels

Cubby™ Productions Inc.
www.cubby198.net

Copyright © 2008 by
Steve Daniels
All rights reserved

Published by Cubby™ Productions Inc.
Sapphire, North Carolina
www.cubby198.net

3rd Printing

Printed in the United States
Cashiers Printing Inc.
Cashiers, North Carolina

No part of this publication may be reproduced, stored in any retrieval system, or transmitted, in any form by any means, electronic, mechanical, photocopying, recording, or otherwise, without the prior written permission of the publisher.

ISBN # 0-971-58144-4

I dedicate this book to my grandson Tyler.
He is very smart and might even be a pilot some day.

Cubby was a bright yellow plane, and unlike most factory built aircraft, he was homebuilt. Created in a garage from scratch, each piece was carefully made by his creator. Because of this, he was labeled, "EXPERIMENTAL," and Cubby loved that. Being an airplane was the greatest thing in the world. He used to be able to fly all day as if the skies belonged to him.

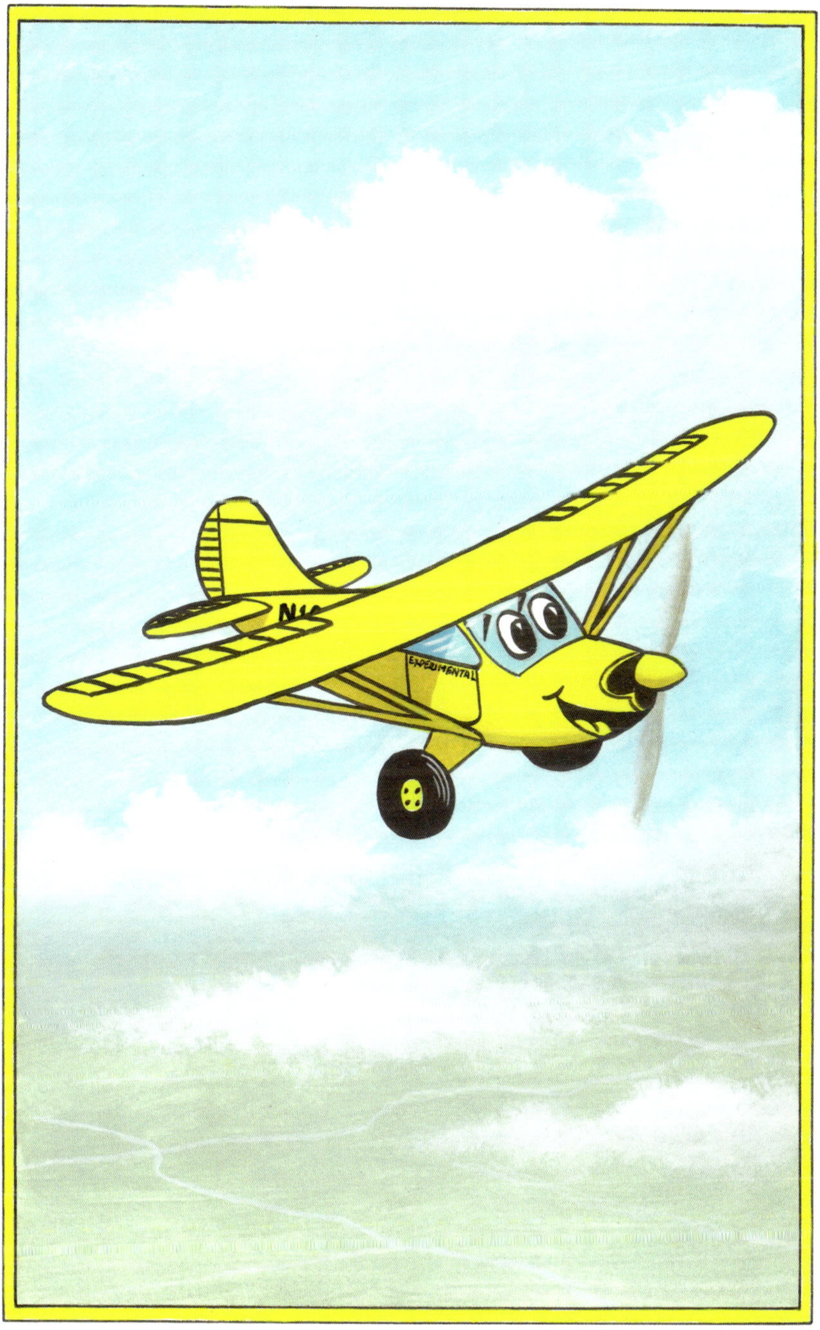
EXPERIMENTAL

Jesse is Cubby's best friend. They were built by the same creator and are both "EXPERIMENTAL."

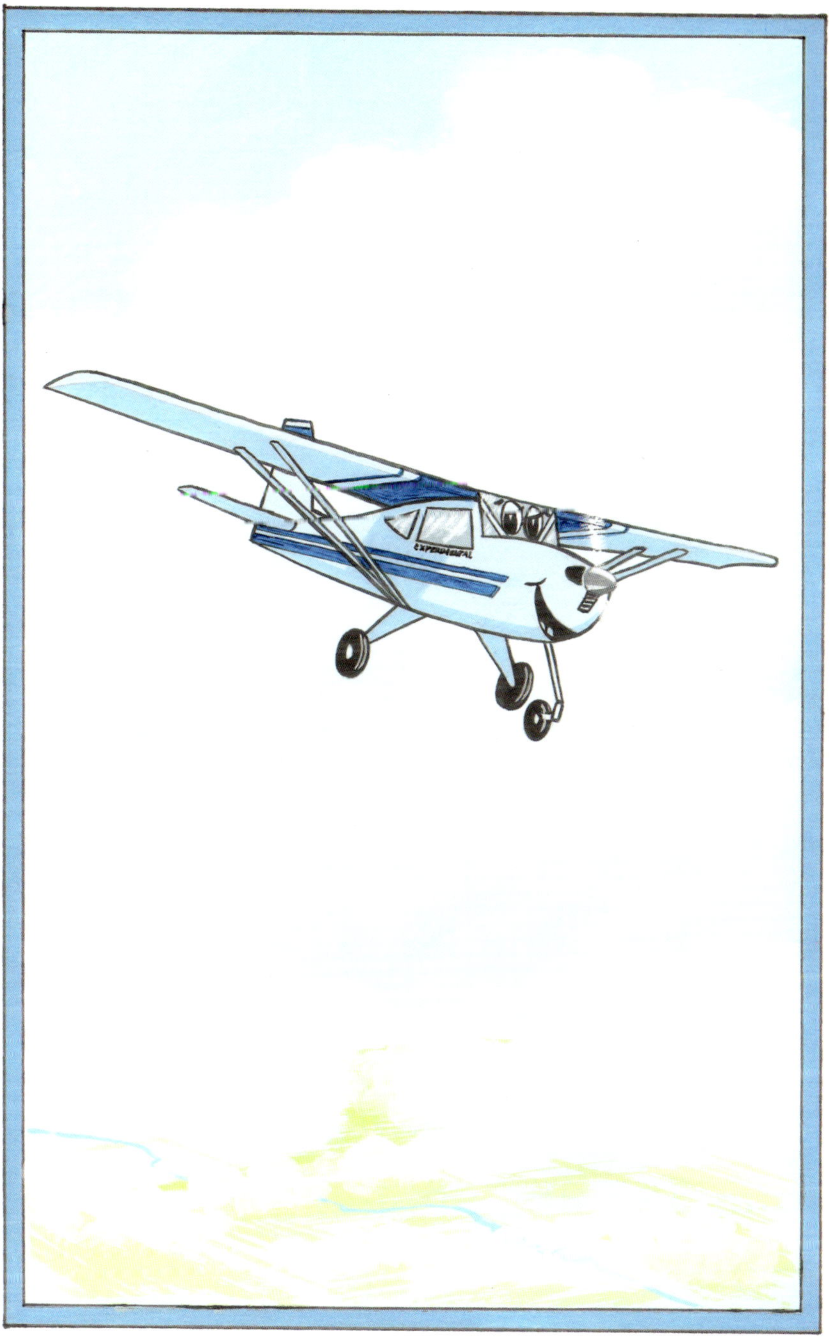

One day while Cubby and Jesse watched the activities around Mountain View Airport,
a beautiful new plane flew in from Canada. Her name was Dominique Diamond and everyone called her "Niki."
It was love at first sight for Cubby. They have been flying together ever since.

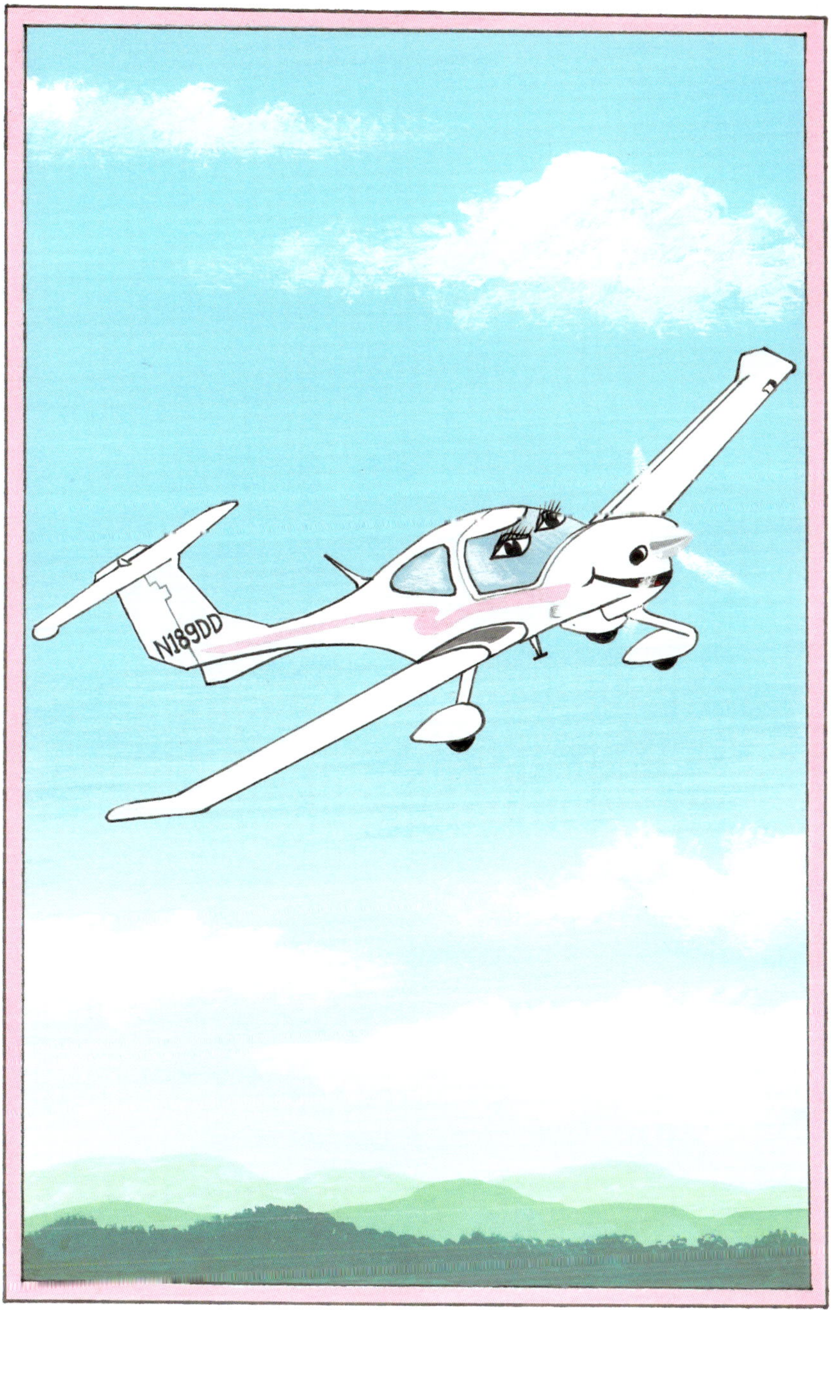
N189DD

There wasn't much room
in the sky for Cubby and his
friends. It was full of big jets
taking people all over the world.
They told Cubby to stay out
of their way.
"They had important things to do."

8

Some of the bigger planes would tell Cubby to get off the runway. They made him feel like he wasn't needed around the airport.

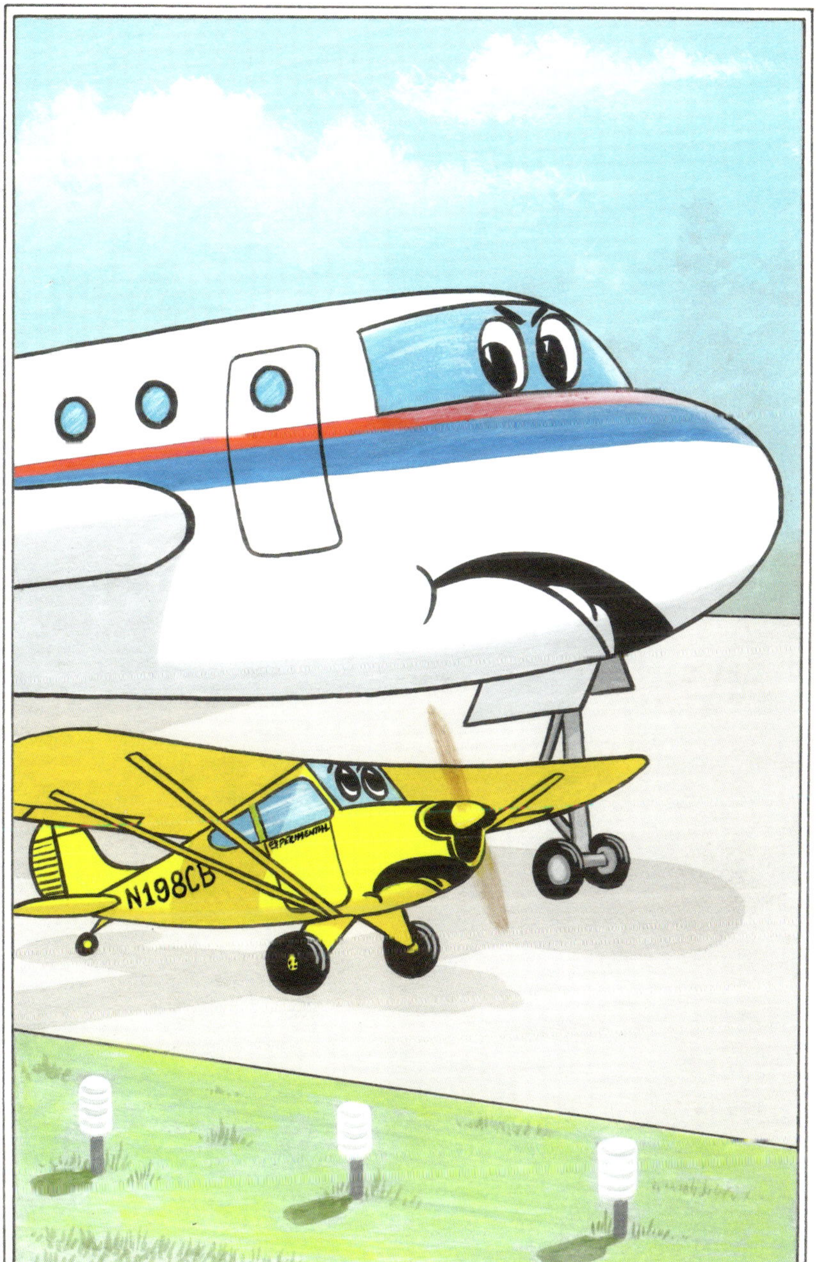
N198CB

Sometimes, when he was able to fly,
one of his friends, "Jet," would sneak
up behind Cubby then pass him.
At first it would scare Cubby, then
they would both laugh.
Have you ever walked up behind
a friend, and jelled "BOO?"
Jet was just having fun with
a good friend.

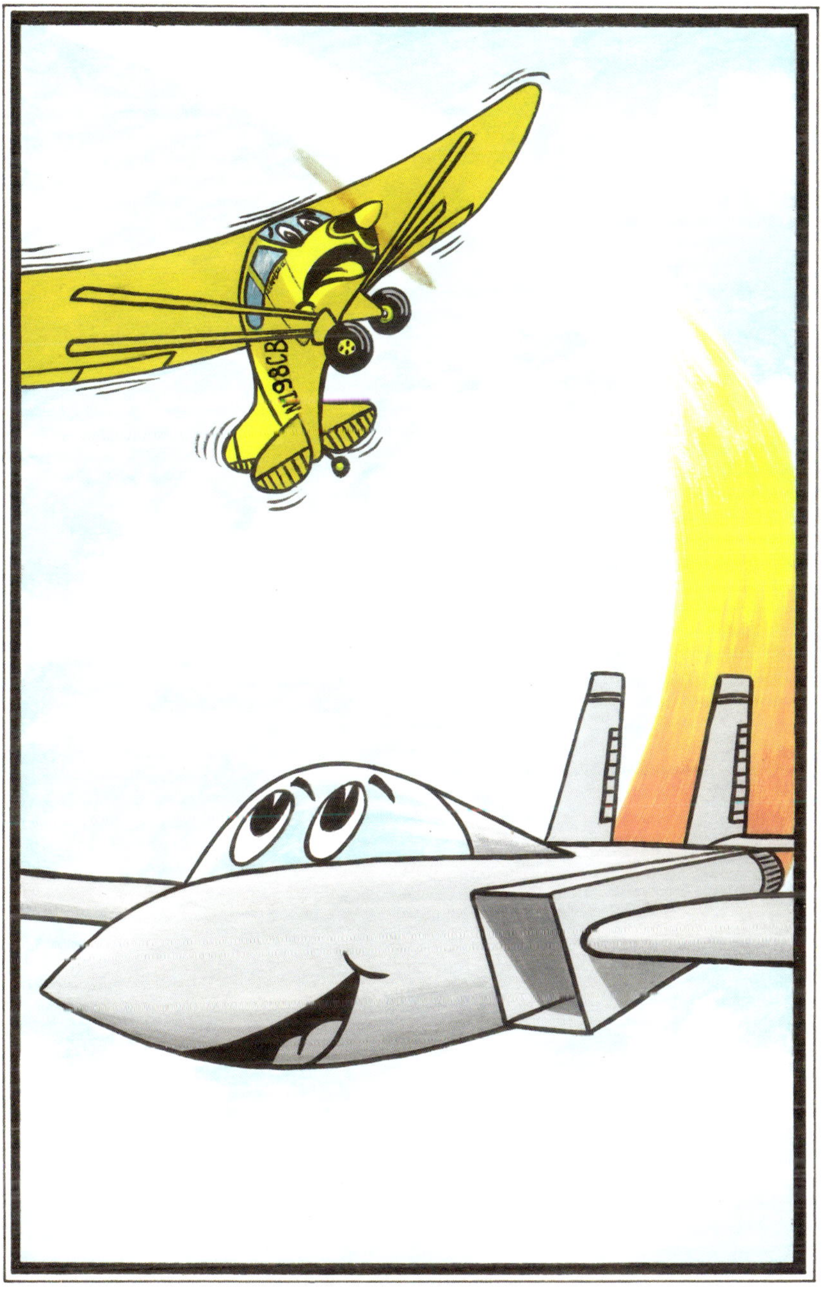
N198CB

Once in a while,
when the big planes were away,
Cubby, Niki, and Jesse
would fly around the clouds
like they were playing
hide and seek.

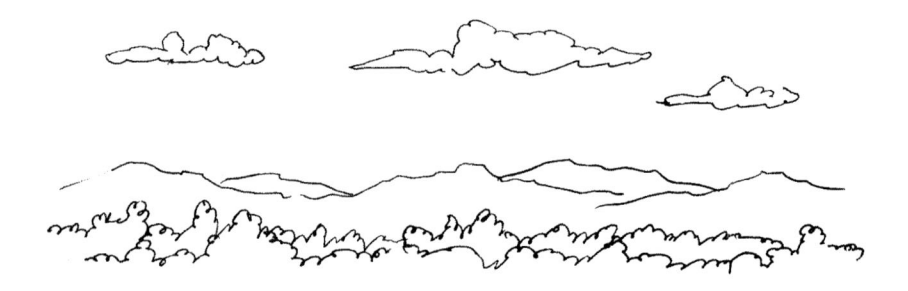

14

One day, Cubby was sitting
in front of his hangar watching
all the activity at the airport,
when suddenly, an ambulance came
through the gate yelling for help.

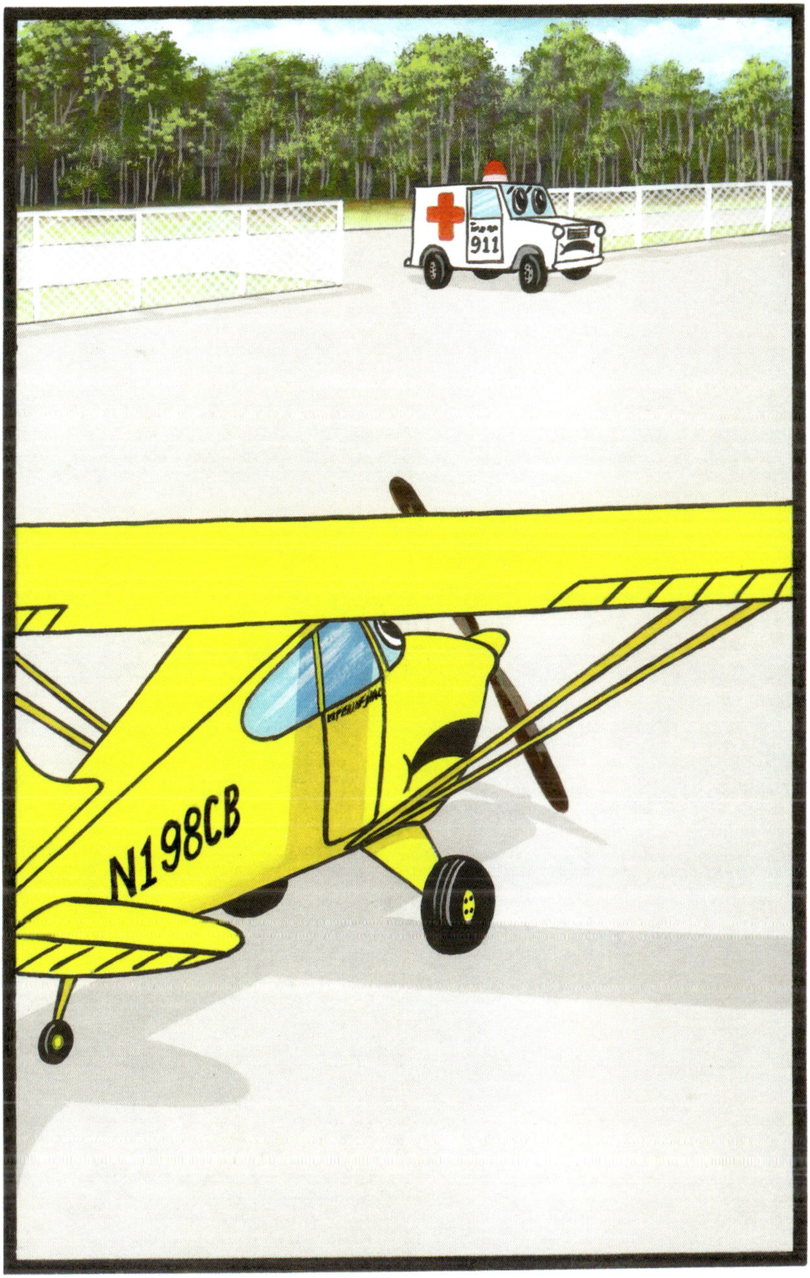
911
N198CB

"Help! Help! I'm carrying a heart that needs to be taken to a small town up north and I can't get through the traffic. The heart is for a transplant for a small child and it needs to get there in a hurry."

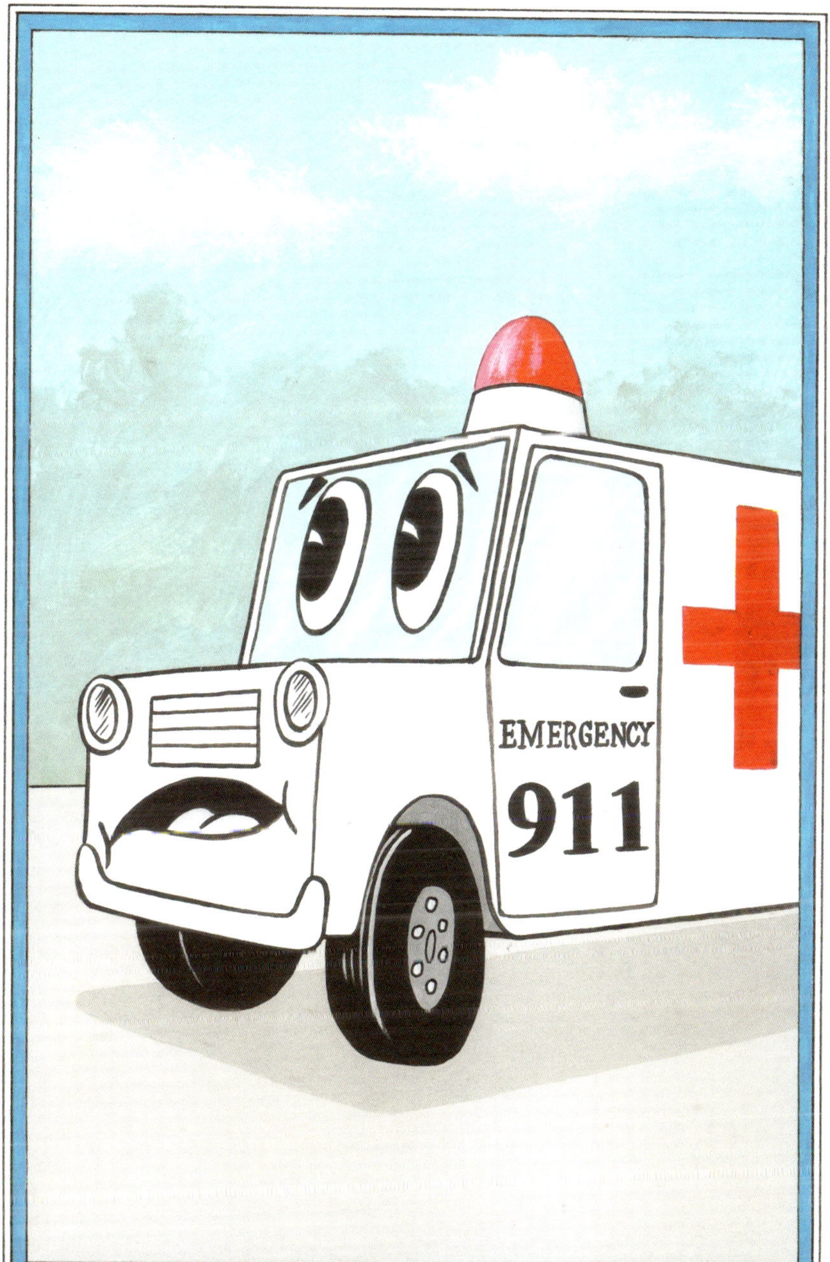
EMERGENCY
911

The big jets said
they couldn't do it because
the runway in the small town
was too short for them.

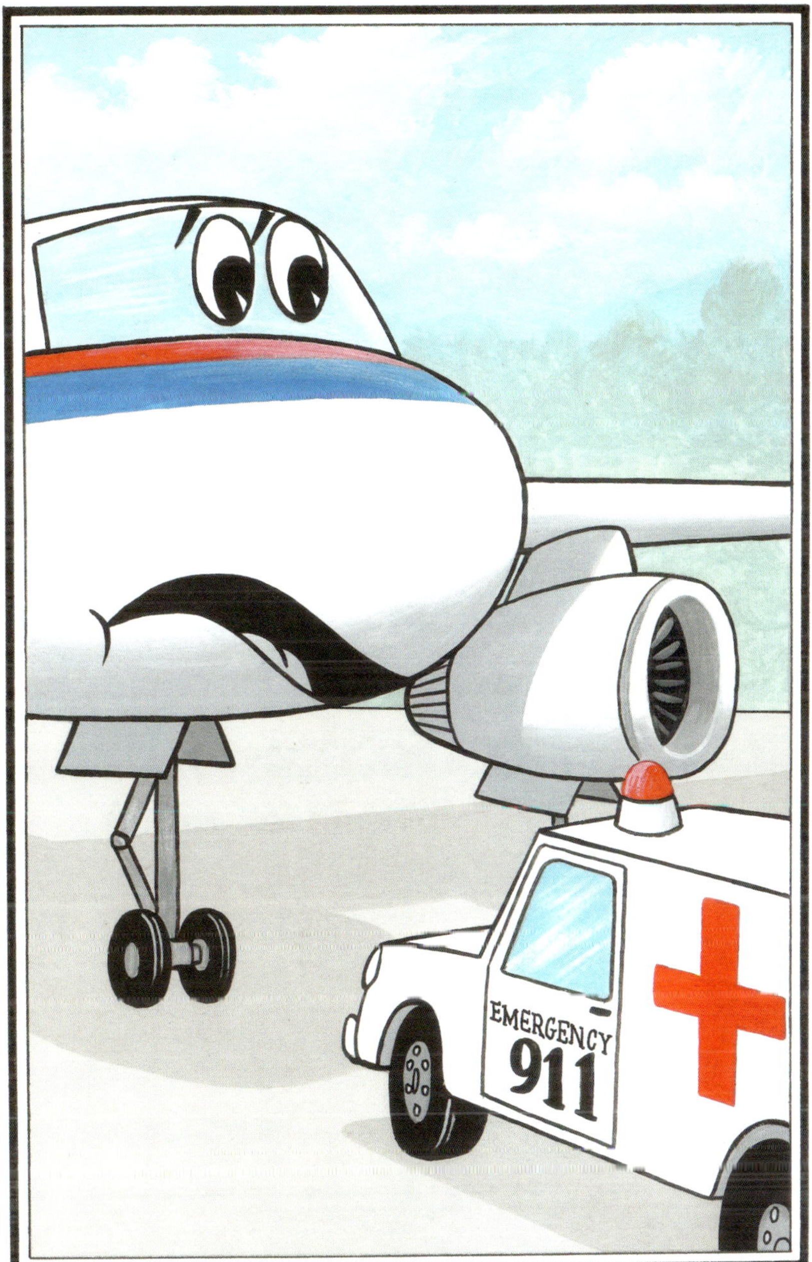
EMERGENCY
911

All the fancy planes said they couldn't do it because the runway in the small town wasn't paved. They couldn't possibly land on grass.

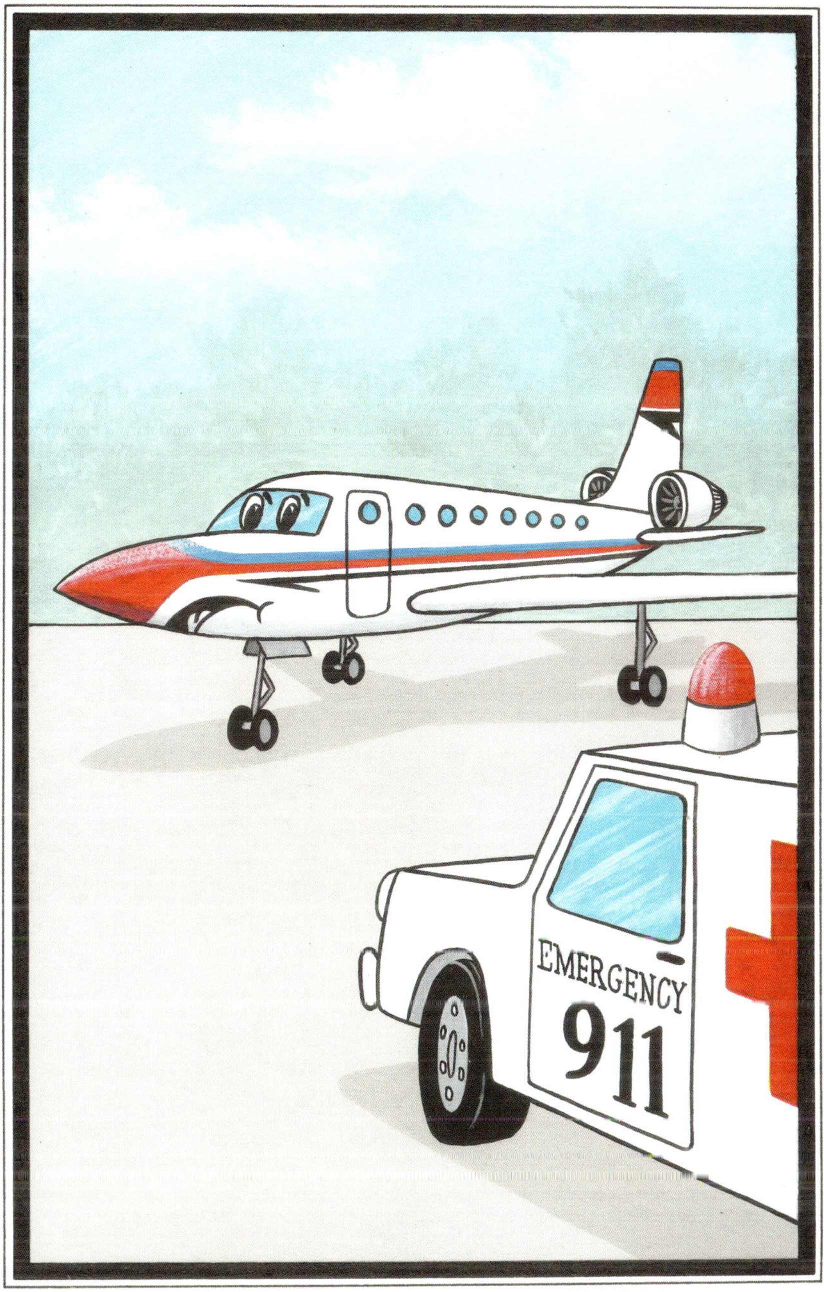
EMERGENCY
911

The news helicopter was far away on a big story and wouldn't be back for a long time.

Niki wasn't able to do the job because the runway wasn't paved and it was built for light sport aircraft. It was just too short for her.

Jesse said he had carburetor trouble and Frank, the mechanic, was going to install a new one soon.

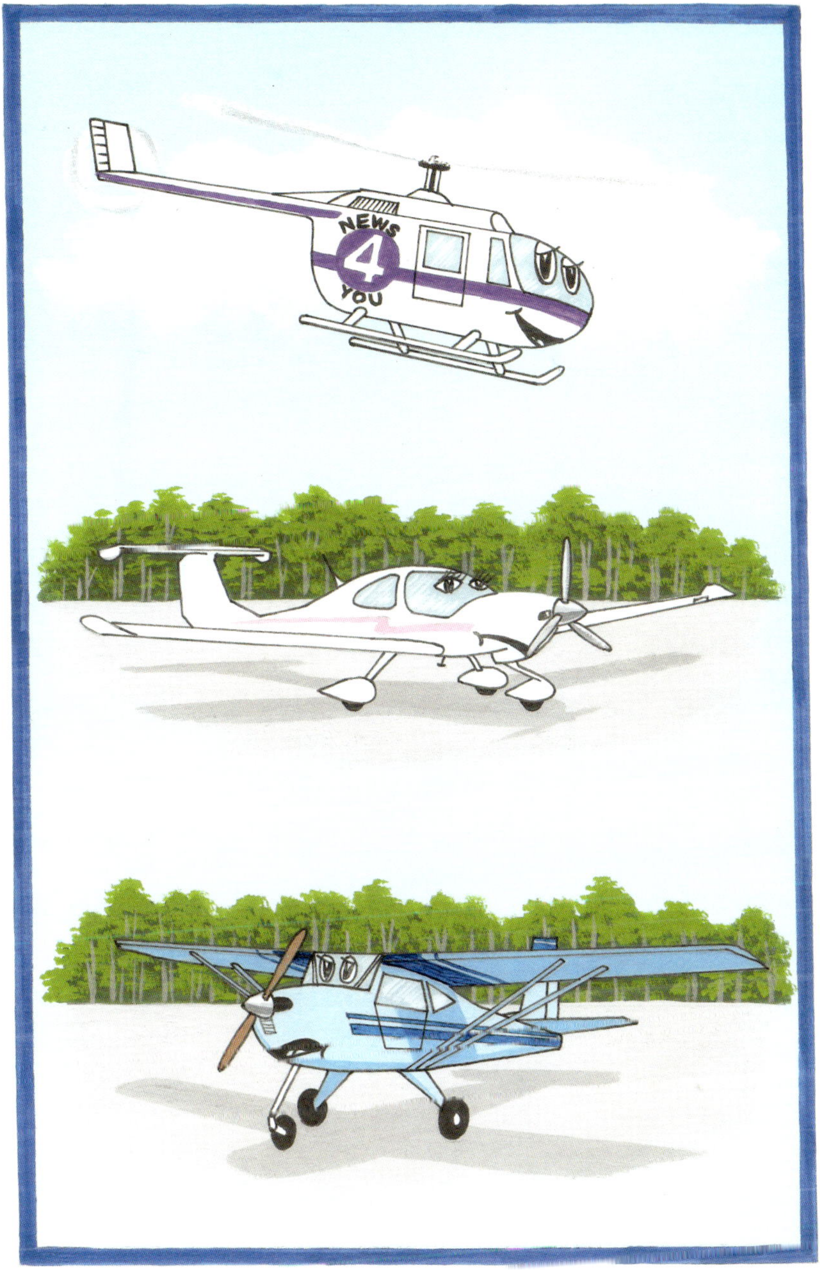
NEWS
4
YOU

Cubby said, I'll do it. I'll take the heart to save the child. That little airport was built for planes like me. It will be great to land on soft grass again. The pavement hurts my wheels."

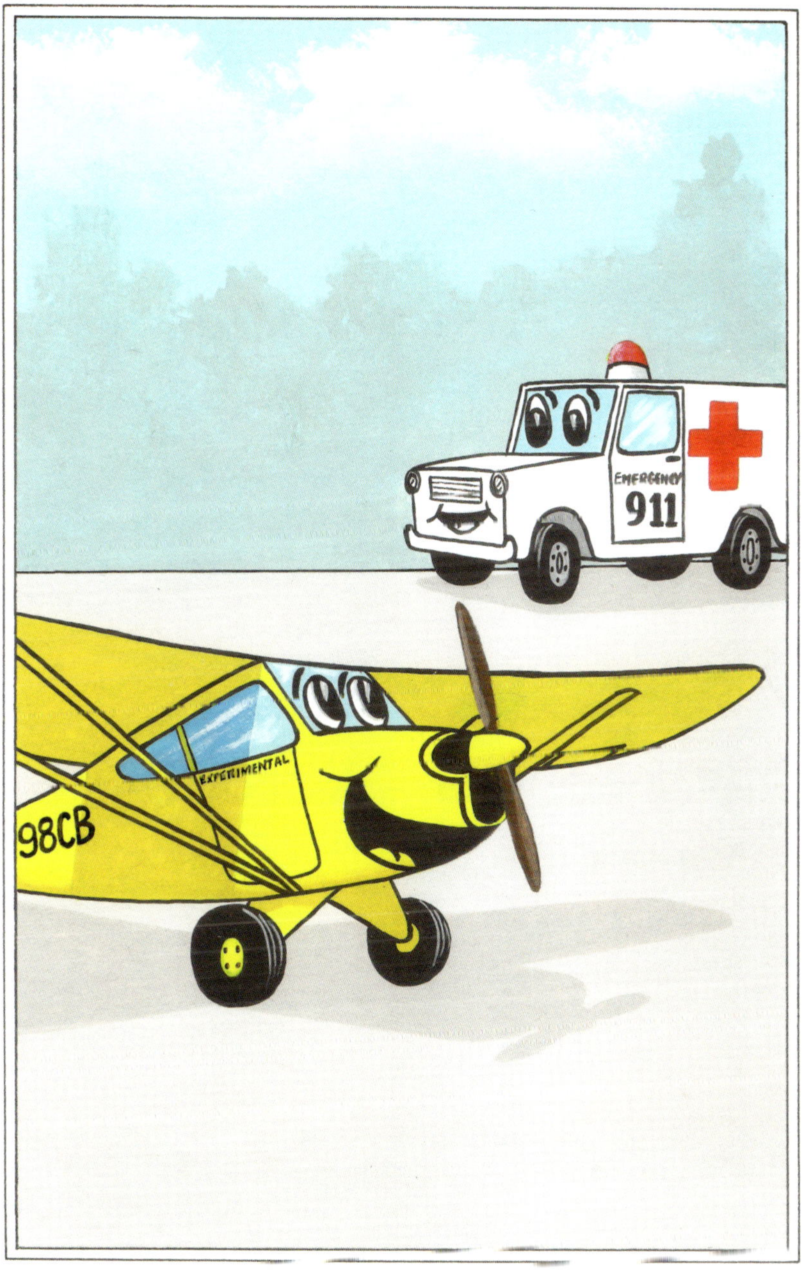
EMERGENCY
911
98CB
EXPERIMENTAL

One of the big jets
laughed and said, "You can't do it.
You are too slow and besides,
you'll get lost."

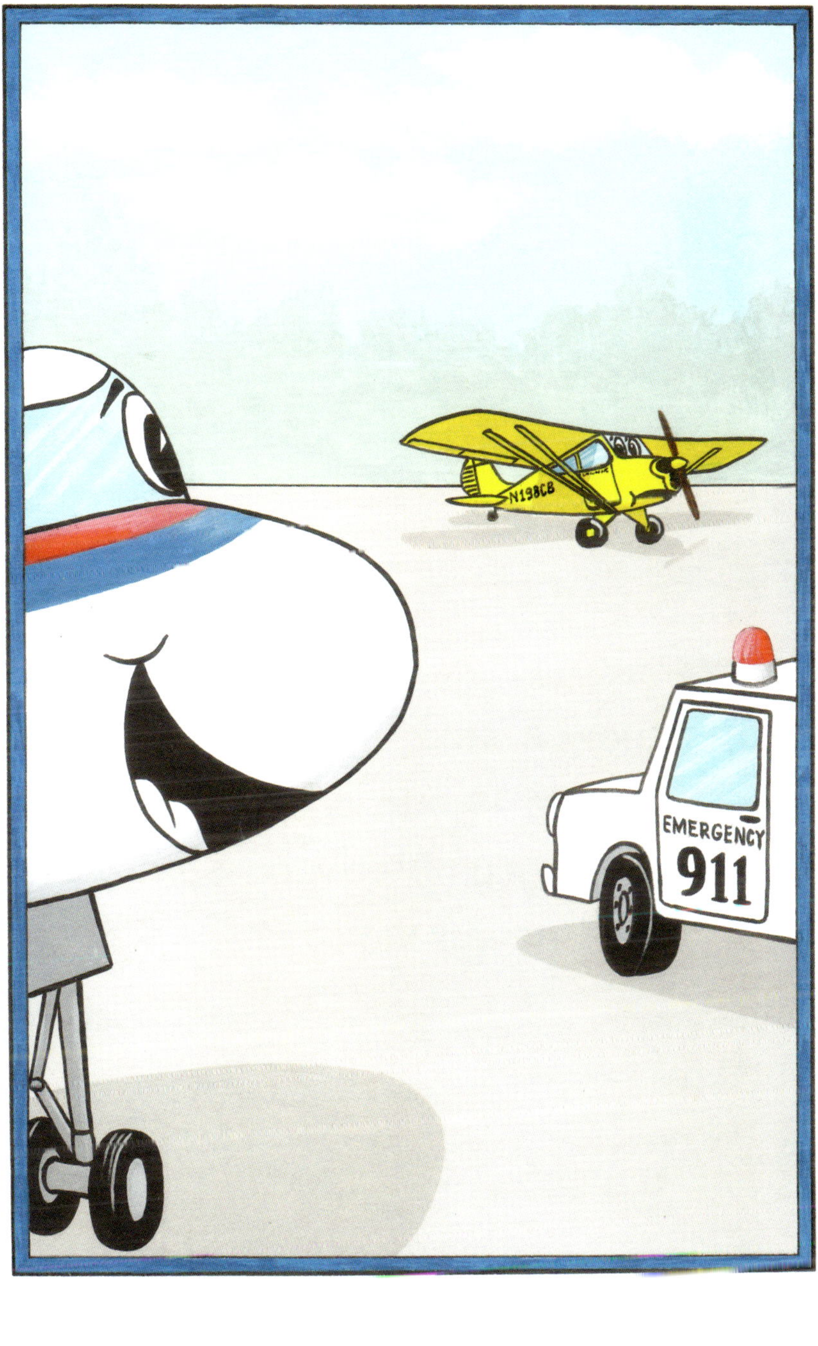
N198CB
EMERGENCY
911

The ambulance said, "Cubby will have to do it. He is our only chance." Another jet grumbled and said, "He will never make it."

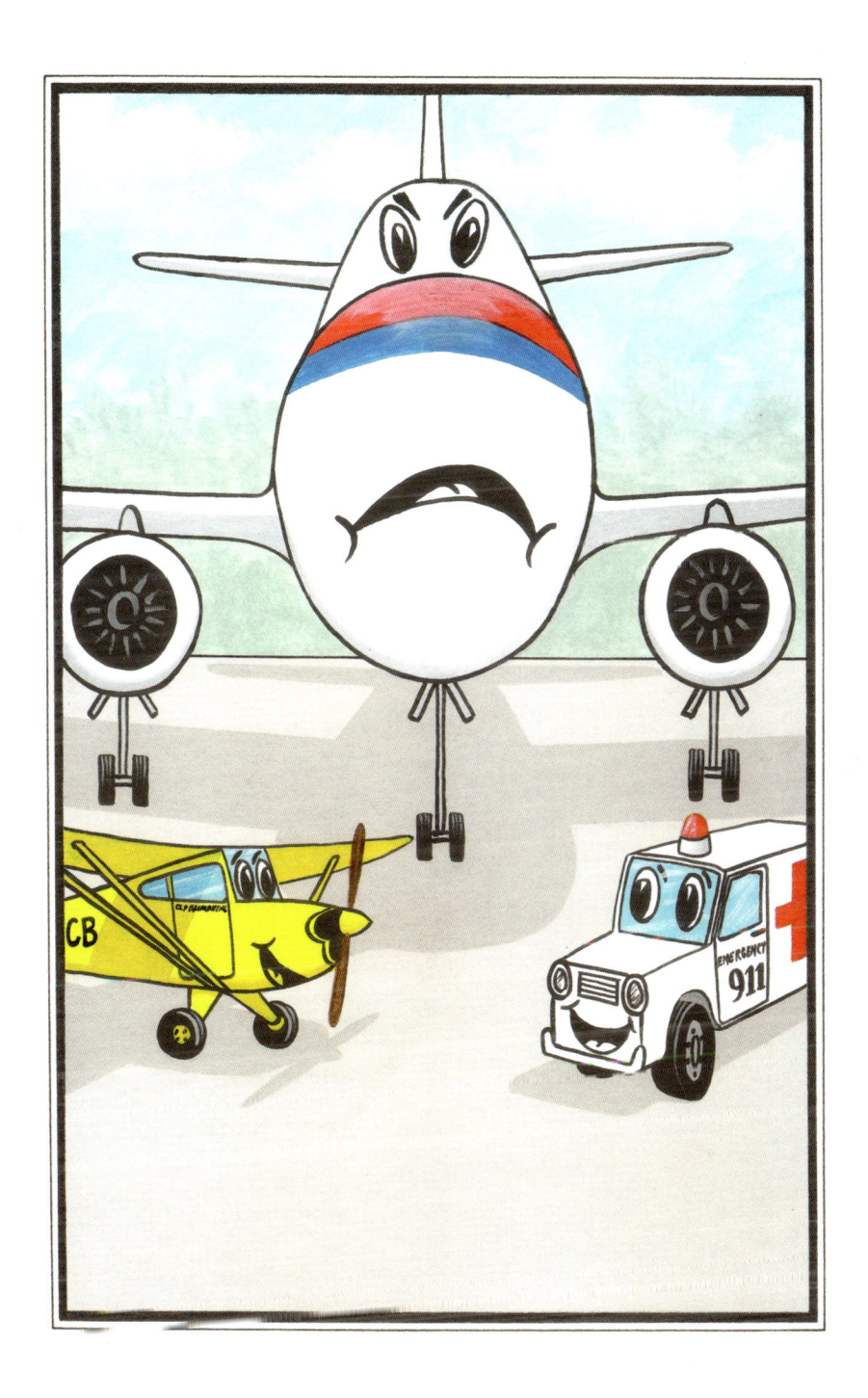
CB
EMERGENCY
911

Cubby proudly rolled up to the ambulance and the heart was given to him. It was packed in a box and the ambulance said, "Fly carefully Cubby, i'ts all up to you now."

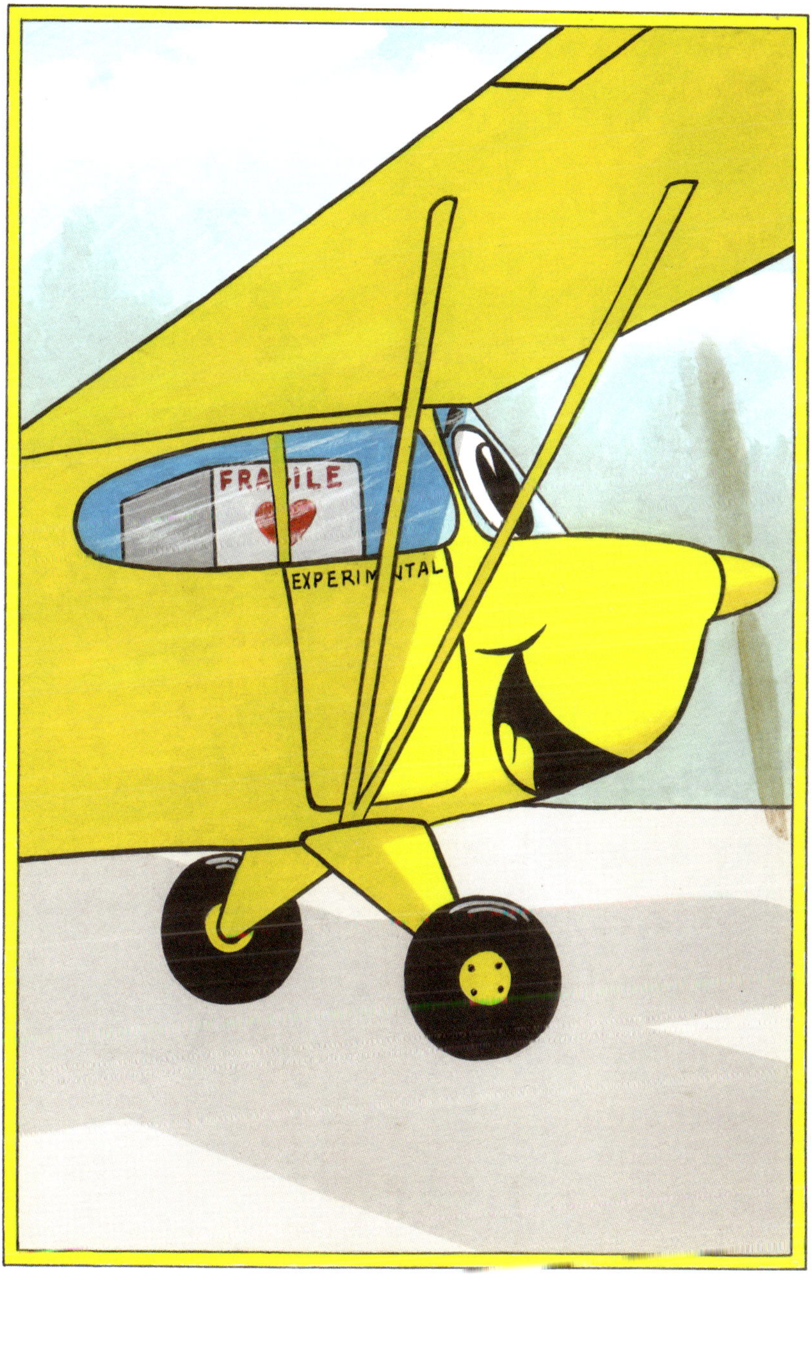
FRAGILE
EXPERIMENTAL

Connie, the control tower,
told all the other planes
to get out of Cubby's way.
They scooted away from him as he
traveled down the runway to take
off. Cubby felt proud. Finally he was
doing something important.
Niki and Jesse told Cubby to,
"Be careful."

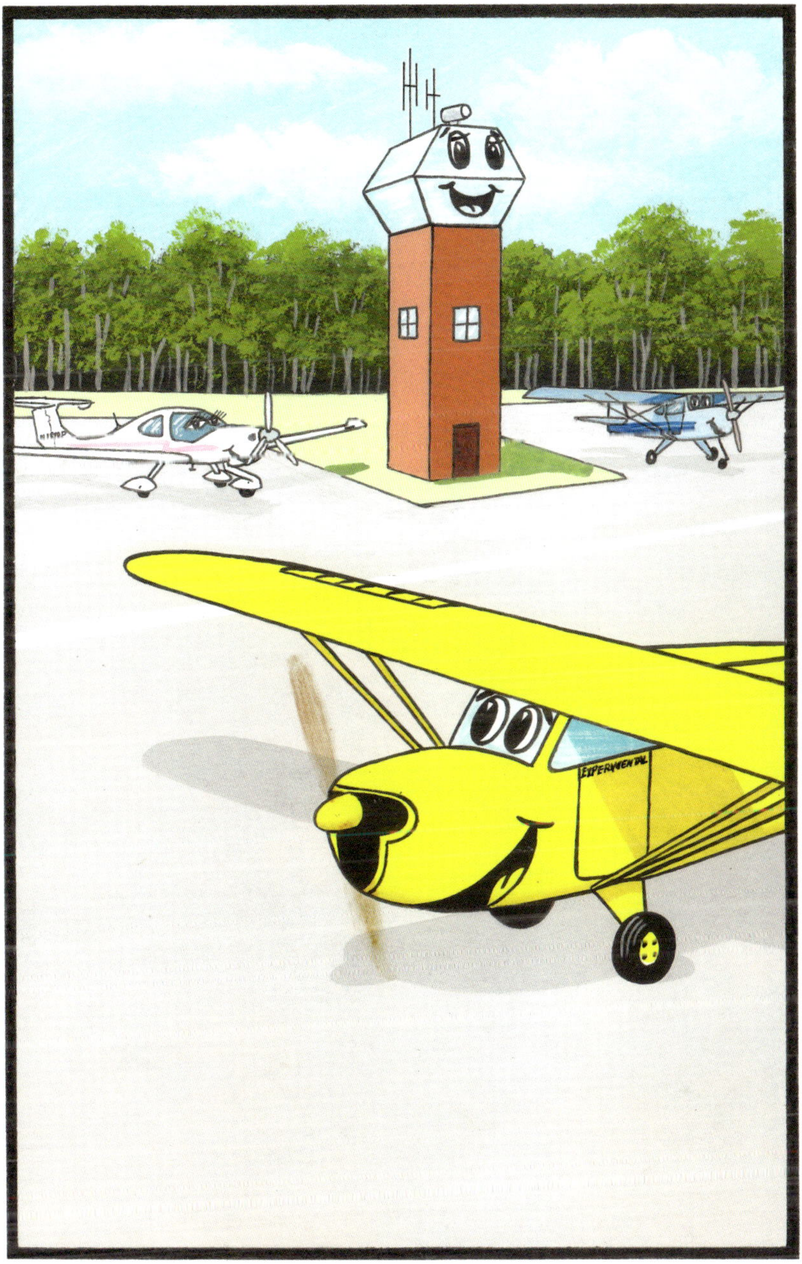
EXPERIMENTAL

As he took off, he turned in the direction of the small town and saw a big storm cloud in his way.
"It's too big to go around so I have to go through it," Cubby said to himself. "This heart must get there as soon as possible."

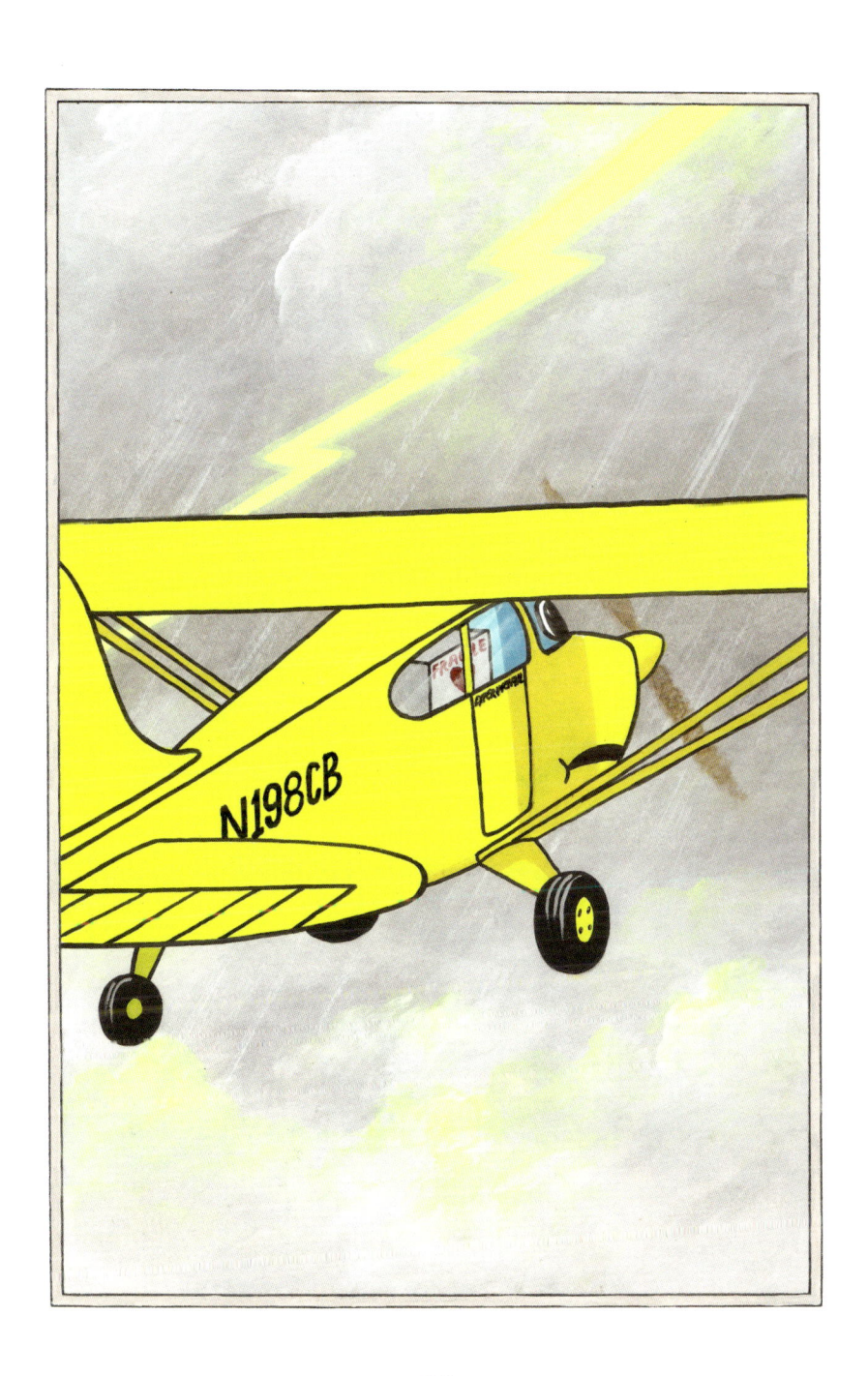
N198CB

The storm tossed and tumbled Cubby and rain beat on his wings as if it didn't want him to get through. It seemed like hours while the storm pounded him, but was only a few minutes.

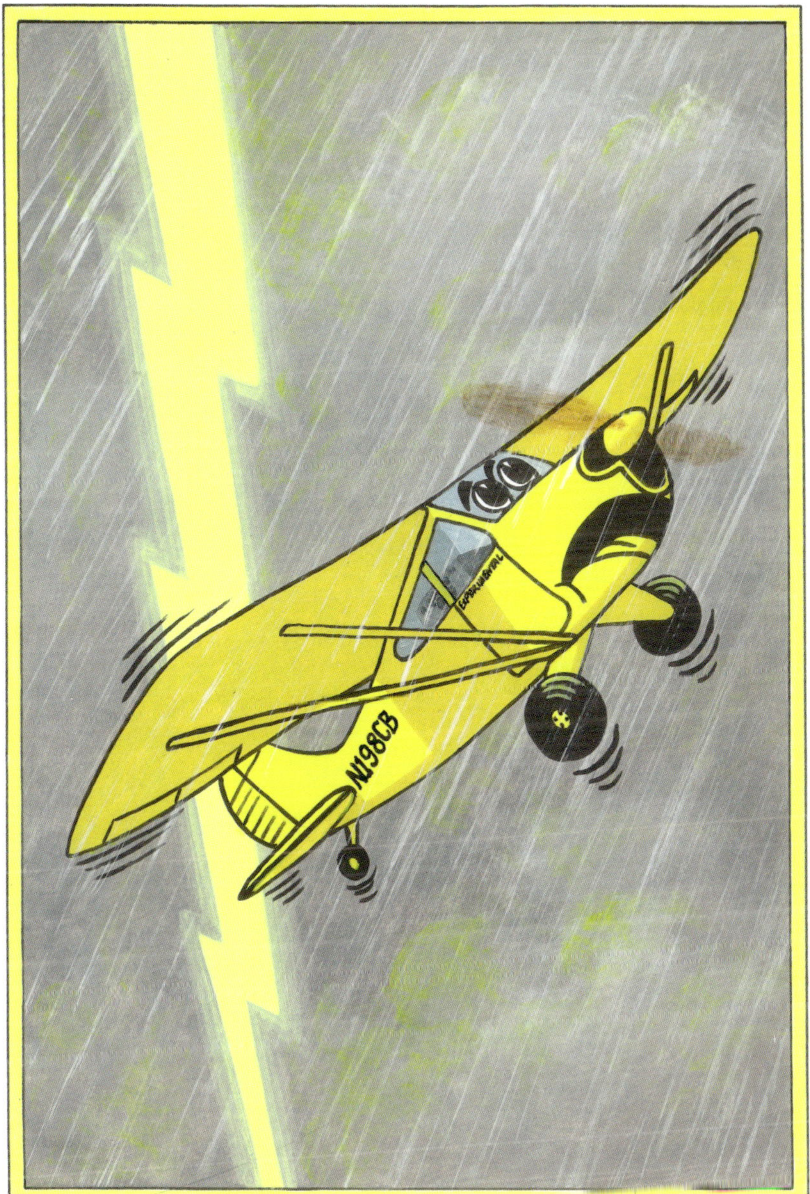
N198CB

Finally, Cubby saw a patch of blue sky and then the ground.

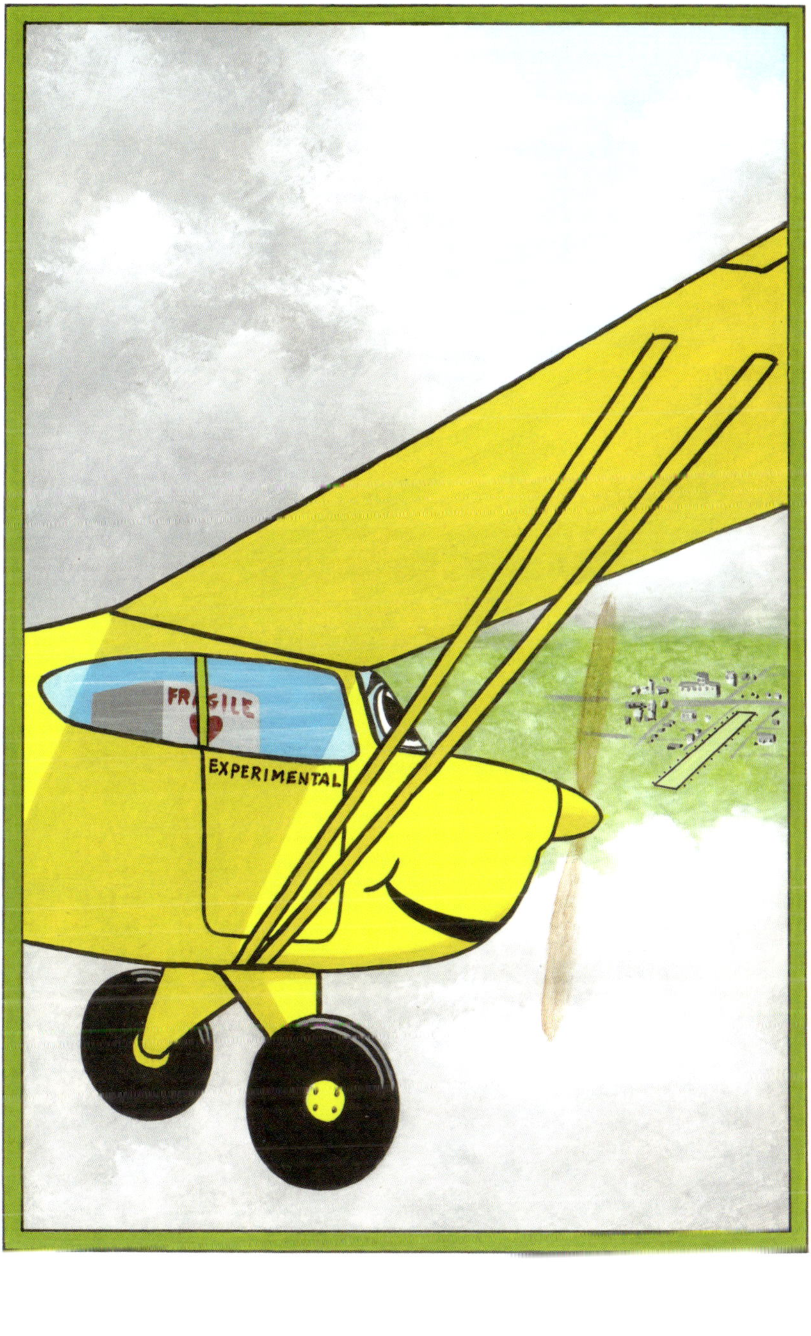
FRAGILE
EXPERIMENTAL

The town was soon in his sight and Cubby spotted the runway. Carefully he came down and touched the grass. "Oh boy!" Cubby shouted. "The grass feels so good and soft." Another ambulance quickly rolled up to him to take the heart to the hospital. "Thank you," said the ambulance. "This heart is just in time to save the life of the child,"

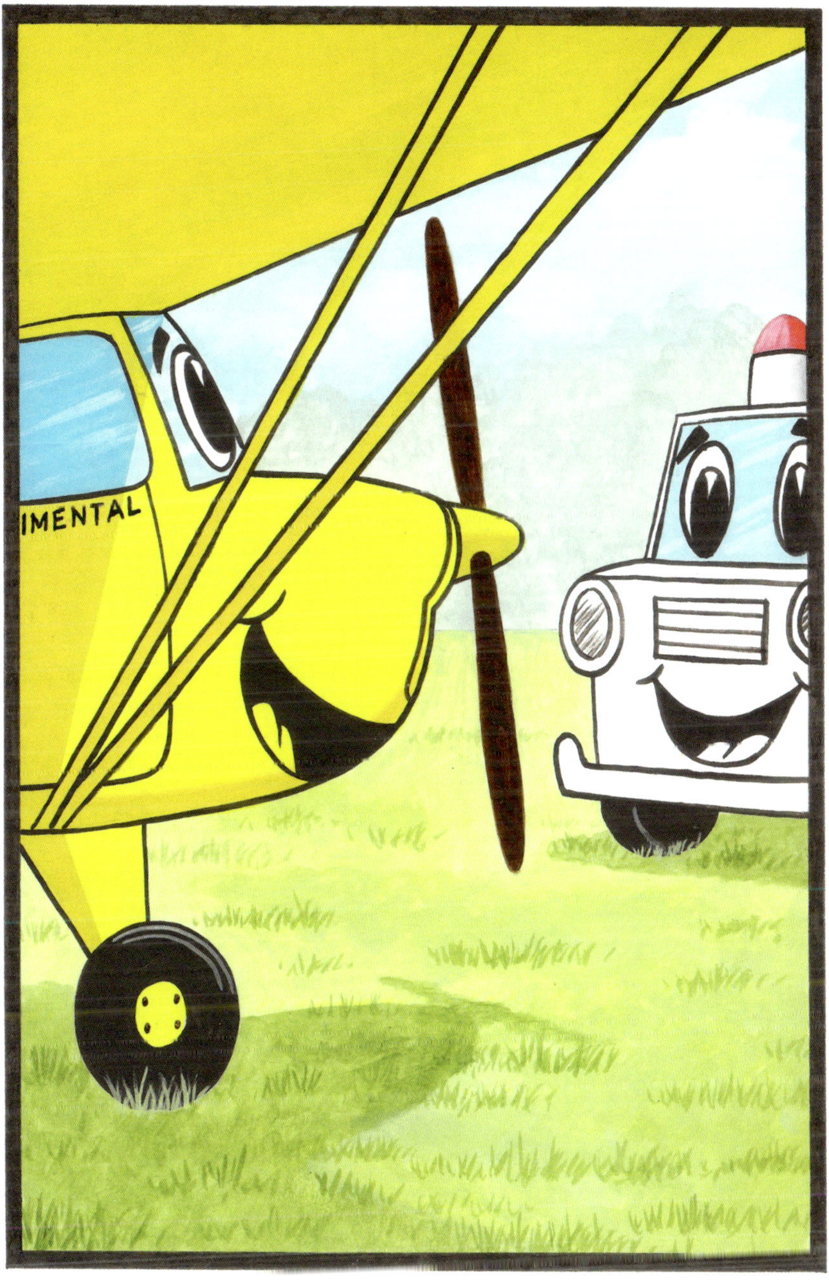
IMENTAL

After watching the ambulance leave the airport, Cubby turned around and took off for home. On his way, the weather was beautiful. Cubby just enjoyed the flight and had a good feeling inside knowing he had helped in an emergency.

When Cubby arrived back home all the planes were lined up on each side of the airport in his honor. He was a hero. A military band played as he traveled to his hangar.

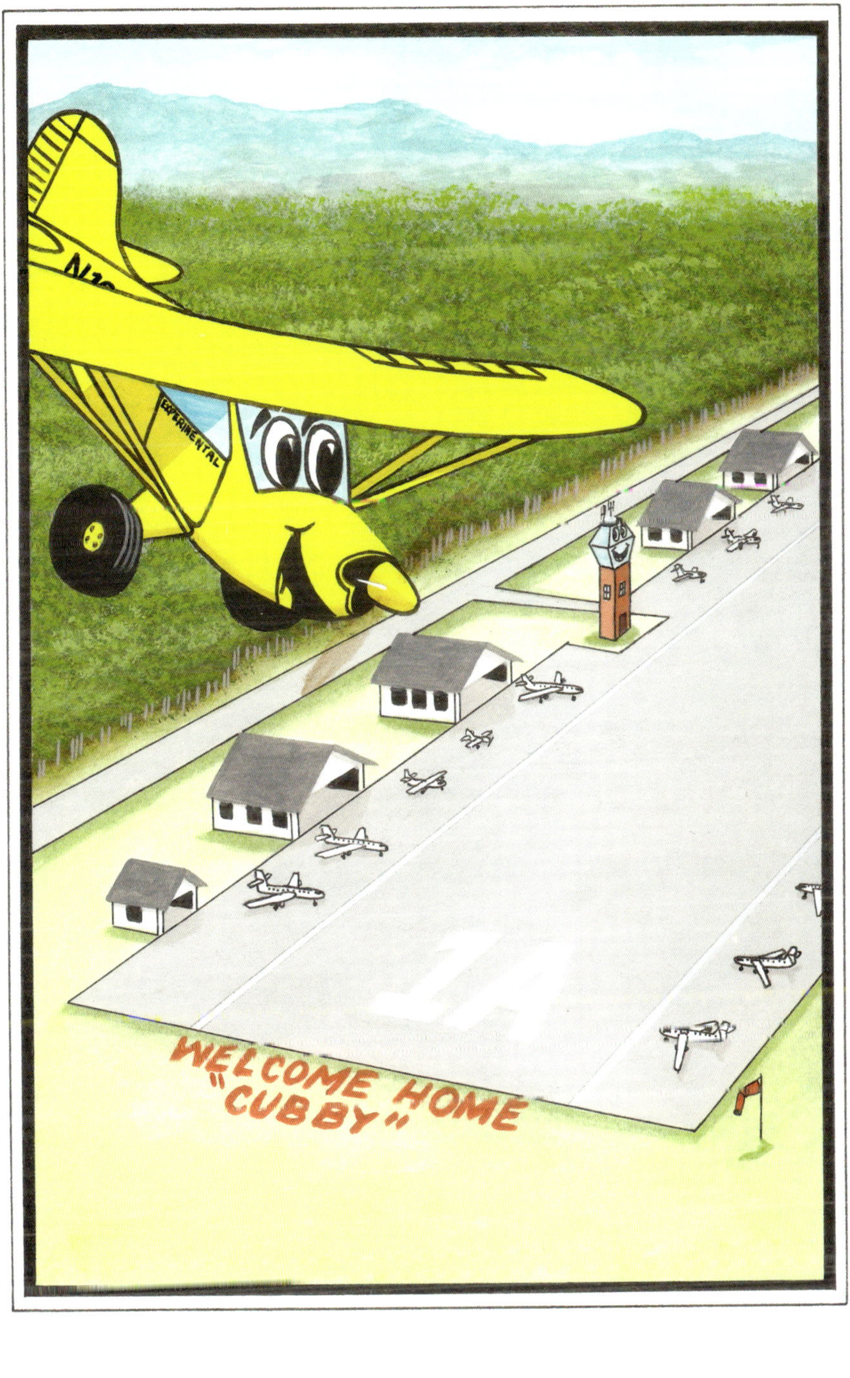
EXPERIMENTAL
14
WELCOME HOME
"CUBBY"

Cubby was honored and that week there was an air show at the airport. Cubby was given a trophy and awarded,
"GRAND CHANPION."

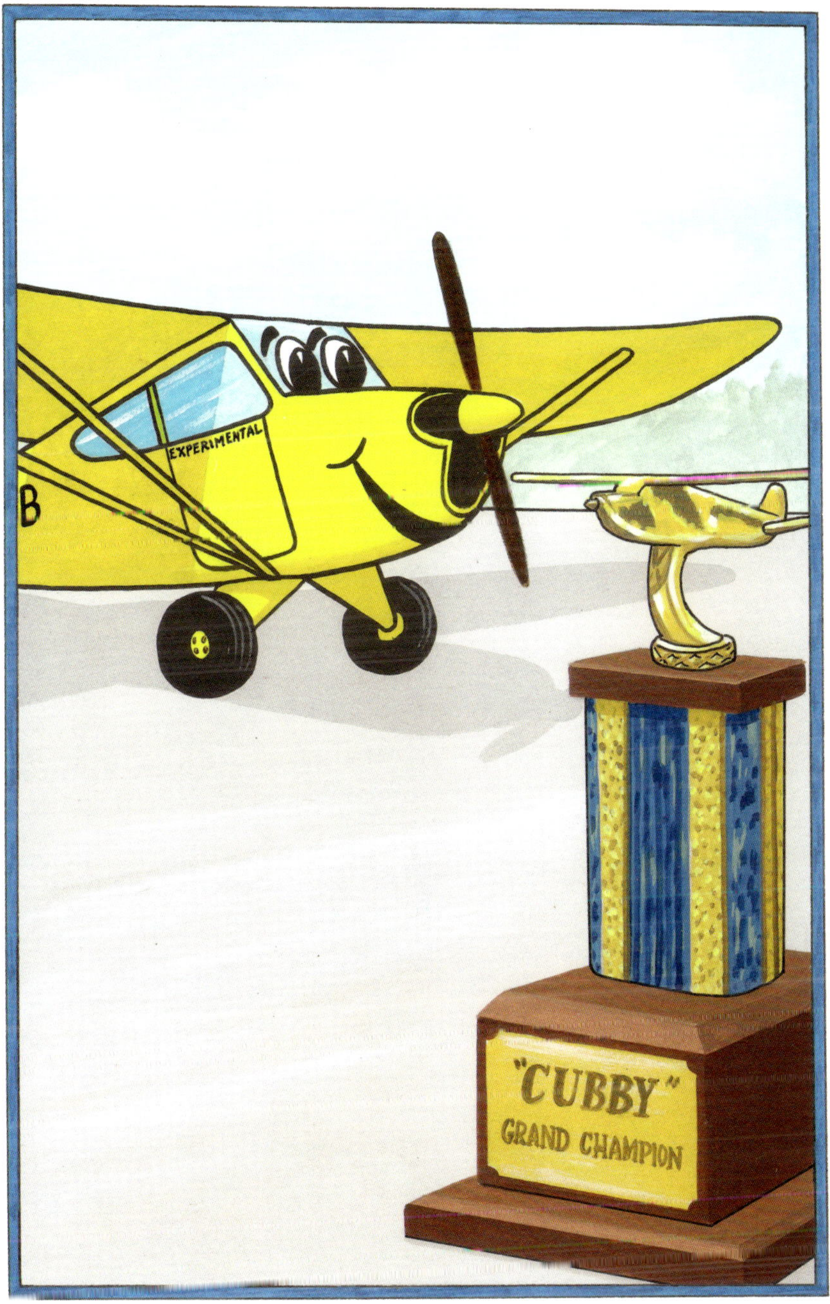
EXPERIMENTAL
"CUBBY"
GRAND CHAMPION

Now Cubby and his friends were allowed to fly any time they wanted and the other planes didn't bother them. The airport even gave Cubby a small grass strip to land on beside the pavement.

"Oh the grass feels so good to my wheels," said Cubby.

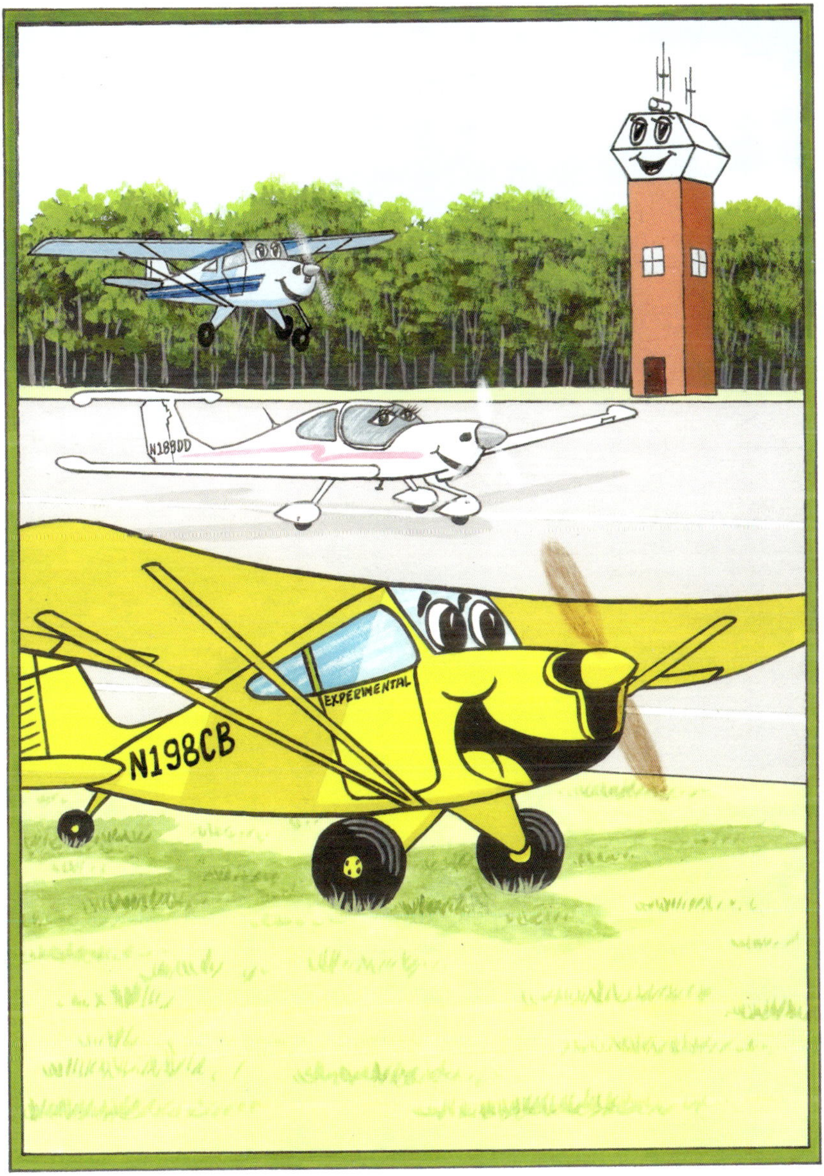
N189DD
EXPERIMENTAL
N198CB

The End